Preface

"AN AMERICAN TRIBUTE" begins in the year 1776 and highlights our historical past together with important current events of our great nation.

Our unique publication is of historical significance with its priceless documents and photographic representations of important events and famous people. It reflects on great deeds by great Americans. The individuals featured and everything illustrated here are symbols of our heritage. As you read and are touched by these most special and most important documents, you will feel a sense of pride with a serene inner peace of mind. The truest expression of freedom and peace is within us. May we honor this value of truth always

As you read THE DECLARATION OF INDEPENDENCE and CONSTITUTION OF THE UNITED STATES OF AMERICA followed by the BILL OF RIGHTS and the GETTYSBURG ADDRESS. you will be inspired to feel the spirit of freedom, and peace, and be proud to be an American. We the people are now and shall always be the thread that bonds freedom and peace into this great nation, THE UNITED STATES OF AMERICA.

All of the representations and illustrations included herein are solely the personal views of the creator of "An American Tribute". As a collectible work of art focused on the historical events of our great nation, we hope you will reflect on and treasure "An American Tribute" as a contribution to and for the preservation of freedom and peace.

May God Bless America.

Richard L. Contreras
Creator of An American Tribute

The focus of this book is on what we felt were the most important symbols that represent our precious country. The individuals featured and everything illustrated here are symbols of our freedom. Freedom, our most important word as Americans. Our country, the United States of America offers us all the right to live free as human beings in a democratic society.

We as Americans need to reflect on this freedom of ours that we so easily take for granted. We should take a hard look at the true heritage that was given to us by our forefathers. Now, more than ever we all need to stand together. It is time for Americans of all origin to come together as one as we say the pledge of allegiance and sing our national anthem. It doesn't matter where we are, in school, at work, or at a special event. We need to let the world hear the voice of freedom ring out. I believe this will unite us once again as Americans and will let the world know who we are. Americans, standing tall and proud and saying thank you to our country and all that it stands for. This is our country built on the faith, courage and the vision of our forefathers for a free nation under God, indivisible, with liberty and justice for all. With the performance of these very thoughts and deeds we shall continue to be the great nation of the United States of America!

Richard L. Contreras

Creator of "An American Tribute"

Table of Contents

Published by Richard L. Contreras
The RILCO Group, Anaheim, California
P.O. Box 1208, Anaheim, CA 92815 / FAX 714-630-0512
Printed in the U.S.A.

U.S. $19.95

Library of Congress Control Number: 2005905752

*"To know our past history
is to learn from it's experiences.
To understand our Constitution
is to preserve our natural freedoms,
and, our inalienable rights to life,
liberty and the pursuit of happiness."*

Richard L. Contreras

"I walk on untrodden ground.
There is scarcely any part of my
conduct that may not hereafter
be drawn into precedent."

G. Washington

George Washington

1732-1783

The Father of Our Country

The first President of our nation, was the foremost person in America during his time. The man on whom the fate of his country depended more than on any other person.

From 1775 to 1783, during the American colonies War of Independence, Washington was Commander-in-Chief of the Continental Army. In the summer of 1787, he presided over America's Constitutional Convention. His presence lent decisive significance to the document drafted there, which continues in force in the twenty-first century as the oldest written constitution in the world. From 1789-1796, he held the highest office in the land as the first president of the United States of America under this constitution. The office of President had in fact been designed with his virtues in mind.

Washington, contributed more to our independence and the enduring union of the American states than anyone of his time. It was in honest recognition of this that history bestowed upon him the epithet "Father of our Country". Upon his death, the memorial address presented on behalf of the Congress of the United States named him "first in war, first in peace, and first in the hearts of his countrymen."

*"I must study politics and war,
that my sons may have the liberty to study
mathematics and philosophy, geography, natural
history, and naval architecture, navigation,
commerce, and agriculture, in order to give their
children a right to study painting, poetry, music,
architecture, statuary, tapestry and porcelain."*

J. Adams

John Adams

1735-1826

2nd President

John Adams was one of our Founding Fathers. He was a member of the Continental congress and served as the very first vice-president of the United States. Adams helped draft the Declaration of Independence and later helped negotiate peace with the British as one of the signers of the Treaty of Paris

John Adams was the first president to occupy the White House. He and his wife Abigail moved in the President's Palace, as it was then known, was still unfinished and littered with debris.

In 1798, Adam's foreign policy averted a war with France. He considered it his greatest accomplishment. He said, "I desire no other inscription over my gravestone than: "Here lies John Adams, who took upon himself the responsibility of the peace with France in the year 1800." He and Jefferson died on the same day, July 4, 1826, the 50th anniversary of the adoption of the Declaration of Independence.

Thomas Jefferson

1743-1826

3rd President

While a member of the Continental Congress Jefferson wrote the Declaration of Independence. Later he was appointed Minister to France. He was appointed Secretary of State in 1790. At the end 1793 he ran for President. Losing to John Adams by three electoral votes, he became Vice President.

Jefferson defeated John Adams in the elections of 1800 becoming the 3d President of the United States of America. He was the undisputed leader of his party known Democratic-Republican. Jefferson was very popular because of his policy of economy and his tax reduction. The most notable achievement of Jefferson's presidency was the Louisiana Purchase in 1803. Acquiring the territory from France doubled the size of the United States.

Jefferson was elected to a second term. Although he was still the undisputed leader of his party, he encountered greater difficulties, on both the domestic and foreign fronts.

After leaving office Jefferson retired to Monticello, his home in Virginia. His last great public service was the founding of the University of Virginia in 1819.

"The happy Union of these States is a wonder; their Constitution a miracle; their example the hope of Liberty throughout the world. Woe to the ambition that would meditate the destruction of either!"

J. Madison

James Madison

1751-1836

4th President

Born in Virginia, James Madison graduated from the College of New Jersey (later Princeton). He was a member of the Virginia convention and framed the Virginia constitution. In 1780 Madison was the youngest delegate chosen to represent Virginia in the Continental Congress.

While in the House of Representatives Madison wrote the Bill of Rights ensuring free speech, press and religion for all U.S. citizens. Like his predecessors, Madison had to deal with the ramifications of European wars. The seizure of our ships, goods, and men on the high seas were a major issue. The country was in a depression. British interference with shipping, as well as other grievances, led to the War of 1812. The war ended in stalemate in December 1814 with the signing of the Treaty of Ghent. American Independence had survived.

Retiring after his second term, Madison continued to be active in public affairs. He served as co-chairman of the Virginia constitutional convention of 1829-30 and rector of the University of Virginia. Although a slaveholder all his life, he became active in the American Colonization Society. The ACS mission was the resettlement of slaves in Africa.

"The American continents, by the free and independent condition which they have assumed and maintain, are henceforth not to be considered as subjects for future colonization by any European Power."

James Monroe

James Monroe

1758-1831

5th President

James Monroe was the last Revolutionary War leader to become president. His entire life was dedicated to serving our country. Monroe's modesty and integrity won him wide esteem and the unwavering loyalty of his friends.

Elected president in 1816 and re-elected in 1820, Monroe's administration was known as the Era of Good Feeling. It was a period of national optimism, expansion, and growth. The greatest legacy of Monroe's presidency was the Monroe Doctrine. It had four main points: (1) The political system of the Americas was different and separate from that of Europe; (2) the Americas were no longer to be regarded as subjects of European colonization; (3) the United States had no intention of interfering with the European "colonies or dependencies" already existing in the Americas; (4) the United States would be hostile to any extension of European power in the Americas.

For more than a century the Monroe doctrine remained the foundation of American foreign policy establishing U.S. interests in the western hemisphere and warning Europe not to attack newly independent South American nations.

"With malice toward none, with charity for all, with firmness in the right as God gives us to see the right, let us strive on to finish the work we are in, to bind up the nation's wounds."

A. Lincoln

Abraham Lincoln

1809-1865

16th President

The son of a Kentucky frontiersman, Lincoln had to struggle for a living and for learning. He studied when ever he could while farming, splitting fence rails, and keeping store at New Salem, Illinois. He spent eight years in the Illinois legislature, and rode the circuit of courts for many years. His law partner said, "His ambition was a little engine that knew no rest.

Lincoln was one of the least popular presidents when elected. Even a supporter called the fanatically honest Illinois lawyer "a first-rate second-rate man." Yet Lincoln proved them wrong as he guided the nation wisely and fairly through the perilous Civil War. Lincoln issued the Emancipation Proclamation in 1863, forever freeing slaves in Confederate territory. Later that year, he delivered his Gettysburg Address on the site of the war's bloodiest battle. He proclaimed that the soldiers did not die in vain, "that this nation, under God, shall have a new birth of freedom — and that government of the people, by the people, for the people, shall not perish from the earth." Finally, in 1865, Confederate troops surrendered at Appomattox, Virginia. Lincoln had generous and conciliatory plans for rebuilding the nation, but he was assassinated by John Wilkes Booth just five days after the surrender.

Signing of the
Declaration of Independence
July 4th, 1776

The Declaration of Independence

IN CONGRESS, July 4, 1776.

The unanimous Declaration of the thirteen united States of America,

(Transcribed from the original text)

When in the Course of human events, it becomes necessary for one people to dissolve the political bands which have connected them with another, and to assume among the powers of the earth, the separate and equal station to which the Laws of Nature and of Nature's God entitle them, a decent respect to the opinions of mankind requires that they should declare the causes which impel them to the separation. We hold these truths to be self-evident, that all men are created equal, that they are endowed by their Creator with certain unalienable Rights, that among these are Life, Liberty and the pursuit of Happiness.--That to secure these rights, Governments are instituted among Men, deriving their just powers from the consent of the governed, --That whenever any Form of Government becomes destructive of these ends, it is the Right of the People to alter or to abolish it, and to institute new Government, laying its foundation on such principles and organizing its powers in such form, as to them shall seem most likely to effect their Safety and Happiness. Prudence, indeed, will dictate that Governments long established should not be changed for light and transient causes; and accordingly all experience hath shewn, that mankind are more disposed to suffer, while evils are sufferable, than to right themselves by abolishing the forms to which they are accustomed. But when a long train of abuses and usurpations, pursuing invariably the same Object evinces a design to reduce them under absolute Despotism, it is their right, it is their duty, to throw off such Government, and to provide new Guards for their future security.--Such has been the patient sufferance of these Colonies; and such is now the necessity which constrains them to alter their former Systems of Government. The history of the present King of Great Britain is a history of repeated injuries and usurpations, all having in direct object the establishment of an absolute Tyranny over these States. To prove this, let Facts be submitted to a candid world.

He has refused his Assent to Laws, the most wholesome and necessary for the public good.

He has forbidden his Governors to pass Laws of immediate and pressing importance, unless suspended in their operation till his Assent should be obtained; and when so suspended, he has utterly neglected to attend to them.

He has refused to pass other Laws for the accommodation of large districts of people, unless those people would relinquish the right of Representation in the Legislature, a right inestimable to them and formidable to tyrants only.

He has called together legislative bodies at places unusual, uncomfortable, and distant from the depository of their public Records, for the sole purpose of fatiguing them into compliance with his measures.

He has dissolved Representative Houses repeatedly, for opposing with manly firmness his invasions on the rights of the people.

He has refused for a long time, after such dissolutions, to cause others to be elected; whereby the Legislative powers, incapable of Annihilation, have returned to the People at large for their exercise; the State remaining in the mean time exposed to all the dangers of invasion from without, and convulsions within.

He has endeavoured to prevent the population of these States; for that purpose obstructing the Laws for Naturalization of Foreigners; refusing to pass others to encourage their migrations hither, and raising the conditions of new Appropriations of Lands.

He has obstructed the Administration of Justice, by refusing his Assent to Laws for establishing Judiciary powers.

He has made Judges dependent on his Will alone, for the tenure of their offices, and the amount and payment of their salaries.

He has erected a multitude of New Offices, and sent hither swarms of Officers to harrass our people, and eat out their substance.

He has kept among us, in times of peace, Standing Armies without the Consent of our legislatures.

He has affected to render the Military independent of and superior to the Civil power.

He has combined with others to subject us to a jurisdiction foreign to our constitution, and unacknowledged by our laws; giving his Assent to their Acts of pretended Legislation:

For Quartering large bodies of armed troops among us: For protecting them, by a mock Trial, from punishment for any Murders which they should commit on the Inhabitants of these States:

For cutting off our Trade with all parts of the world: For imposing Taxes on us without our Consent: For depriving us in many cases, of the benefits of Trial by Jury: For transporting us beyond Seas to be tried for pretended offences

For abolishing the free System of English Laws in a neighbouring Province, establishing therein an Arbitrary government, and enlarging its Boundaries so as to render it at once an example and fit instrument for introducing the same absolute rule into these Colonies:

For taking away our Charters, abolishing our most valuable Laws, and altering fundamentally the Forms of our Governments:

For suspending our own Legislatures, and declaring themselves invested with power to legislate for us in all cases whatsoever.

He has abdicated Government here, by declaring us out of his Protection and waging War against us.

He has plundered our seas, ravaged our Coasts, burnt our towns, and destroyed the lives of our people.

He is at this time transporting large Armies of foreign Mercenaries to compleat the works of death, desolation and tyranny, already begun with circumstances of Cruelty & perfidy scarcely paralleled in the most barbarous ages, and totally unworthy the Head of a civilized nation.

He has constrained our fellow Citizens taken Captive on the high Seas to bear Arms against their Country, to become the executioners of their friends and Brethren, or to fall themselves by their Hands.

He has excited domestic insurrections amongst us, and has endeavoured to bring on the inhabitants of our frontiers, the merciless Indian Savages, whose known rule of warfare, is an undistinguished destruction of all ages, sexes and conditions.

In every stage of these Oppressions We have Petitioned for Redress in the most humble terms: Our repeated Petitions have been answered only by repeated injury. A Prince whose character is thus marked by every act which may define a Tyrant, is unfit to be the ruler of a free people.

Nor have We been wanting in attentions to our Brittish brethren. We have warned them from time to time of attempts by their legislature to extend an unwarrantable jurisdiction over us. We have reminded them of the circumstances of our emigration and settlement here. We have appealed to their native justice and magnanimity, and we have conjured them by the ties of our common kindred to disavow these usurpations, which, would inevitably interrupt our connections and correspondence. They too have been deaf to the voice of justice and of consanguinity. We must, therefore, acquiesce in the necessity, which denounces our Separation, and hold them, as we hold the rest of mankind, Enemies in War, in Peace Friends.

We, therefore, the Representatives of the united States of America, in General Congress, Assembled, appealing to the Supreme Judge of the world for the rectitude of our intentions, do, in the Name, and by Authority of the good People of these Colonies, solemnly publish and declare, That these United Colonies are, and of Right ought to be Free and Independent States; that they are Absolved from all Allegiance to the British Crown, and that all political connection between them and the State of Great Britain, is and ought to be totally dissolved; and that as Free and Independent States, they have full Power to levy War, conclude Peace, contract Alliances, establish Commerce, and to do all other Acts and Things which Independent States may of right do. And for the support of this Declaration, with a firm reliance on the protection of divine Providence, we mutually pledge to each other our Lives, our Fortunes and our sacred Honor.

Signed by every member of the Contintial Congress
July 4th, 1776 at the risk of prosecution
for treason by the British Government.

Constitution of the United States of America

(Note: The following text is a transcription of the Constitution in its original form.)

We the People of the United States, in Order to form a more perfect Union, establish Justice, insure domestic Tranquility, provide for the common defense, promote the general Welfare, and secure the Blessings of Liberty to ourselves and our Posterity, do ordain and establish this Constitution for the United States of America.

Article. I.

Section. 1. All legislative Powers herein granted shall be vested in a Congress of the United States, which shall consist of a Senate and House of Representatives.

Section. 2. The House of Representatives shall be composed of Members chosen every second Year by the People of the several States, and the Electors in each State shall have the Qualifications requisite for Electors of the most numerous Branch of the State Legislature.

No Person shall be a Representative who shall not have attained to the Age of twenty five Years, and been seven Years a Citizen of the United States, and who shall not, when elected, be an Inhabitant of that State in which he shall be chosen.

Representatives and direct Taxes shall be apportioned among the several States which may be included within this Union, according to their respective Numbers, which shall be determined by adding to the whole Number of free Persons, including those bound to Service for a Term of Years, and excluding Indians not taxed, three fifths of all other Persons. The actual Enumeration shall be made within three Years after the first Meeting of the Congress of the United States, and within every subsequent Term of ten Years, in such Manner as they shall by Law direct. The Number of Representatives shall not exceed one for every thirty Thousand, but each State shall have at Least one Representative; and until such enumeration shall be made, the State of New Hampshire shall be entitled to chuse three, Massachusetts eight, Rhode-Island and Providence Plantations one, Connecticut five, New-York six, New Jersey four, Pennsylvania eight, Delaware one, Maryland six, Virginia ten, North Carolina five, South Carolina five, and Georgia three.

When vacancies happen in the Representation from any State, the Executive Authority thereof shall issue Writs of Election to fill such Vacancies.

The House of Representatives shall chuse their Speaker and other Officers; and shall have the sole Power of Impeachment.

Section. 3. The Senate of the United States shall be composed of two Senators from each State, chosen by the Legislature thereof for six Years; and each Senator shall have one Vote. Immediately after they shall be assembled in Consequence of the first Election, they shall be divided as equally as may be into three Classes. The Seats of the Senators of the first Class shall be vacated at the Expiration of the second Year, of the second Class at the Expiration of the fourth Year, and of the third Class at the Expiration of the sixth Year, so that one third may be chosen every second Year; and if Vacancies happen by Resignation, or otherwise, during the Recess of the Legislature of any State, the Executive thereof may make temporary Appointments until the next Meeting of the Legislature, which shall then fill such Vacancies.

No Person shall be a Senator who shall not have attained to the Age of thirty Years, and been nine Years a Citizen of the United States, and who shall not, when elected, be an Inhabitant of that State for which he shall be chosen.

The Vice President of the United States shall be President of the Senate, but shall have no Vote, unless they be equally divided.

The Senate shall chuse their other Officers, and also a President pro tempore, in the Absence of the Vice President, or when he shall exercise the Office of President of the United States.

The Senate shall have the sole Power to try all Impeachments. When sitting for that Purpose, they shall be on Oath or Affirmation. When the President of the United States is tried, the Chief Justice shall preside: And no Person shall be convicted without the Concurrence of two thirds of the Members present.

Judgment in Cases of Impeachment shall not extend further than to removal from Office, and disqualification to hold and enjoy any Office of honor, Trust or Profit under the United States: but the Party convicted shall nevertheless be liable and subject to Indictment, Trial, Judgment and Punishment, according to Law.

Section. 4. The Times, Places and Manner of holding Elections for Senators and Representatives, shall be prescribed in each State by the Legislature thereof; but the Congress may at any time by Law make or alter such Regulations, except as to the Places of chusing Senators.

The Congress shall assemble at least once in every Year, and such Meeting shall be on the first Monday in December, unless they shall by Law appoint a different Day.

Section. 5. Each House shall be the Judge of the Elections, Returns and Qualifications of its own Members, and a Majority of each shall constitute a Quorum to do Business; but a smaller Number may adjourn from day to day, and may be authorized to compel the Attendance of absent Members, in such Manner, and under such Penalties as each House may provide.

Each House may determine the Rules of its Proceedings, punish its Members for disorderly Behaviour, and, with the Concurrence of two thirds, expel a Member.

Each House shall keep a Journal of its Proceedings, and from time to time publish the same, excepting such Parts as may in their Judgment require Secrecy; and the Yeas and Nays of the Members of either House on any question shall, at the Desire of one fifth of those Present, be entered on the Journal.

Neither House, during the Session of Congress, shall, without the Consent of the other, adjourn for more than three days, nor to any other Place than that in which the two Houses shall be sitting.

Section. 6. The Senators and Representatives shall receive a Compensation for their Services, to be ascertained by Law, and paid out of the Treasury of the United States. They shall in all Cases, except Treason, Felony and Breach of the Peace, be privileged from Arrest during their Attendance at the Session of their respective Houses, and in going to and returning from the same; and for any Speech or Debate in either House, they shall not be questioned in any other Place.

No Senator or Representative shall, during the Time for which he was elected, be appointed to any civil Office under the Authority of the United States, which shall have been created, or the moluments whereof shall have been encreased during such time; and no Person holding any Office under the United States, shall be a Member of either House during his Continuance in Office.

Section. 7. All Bills for raising Revenue shall originate in the House of Representatives; but the Senate may propose or concur with Amendments as on other Bills.

Every Bill which shall have passed the House of Representatives and the Senate, shall, before it become a Law, be presented to the President of the United States: If he approve he shall sign it, but if not he shall return it, with his Objections to that House in which it shall have originated, who shall enter the Objections at large on their Journal, and proceed to reconsider it. If after such reconsideration two thirds of that House shall agree to pass the Bill, it shall be sent, together with the Objections, to the other House, by which it shall likewise be reconsidered, and if approved by two thirds of that House, it shall become a Law. But in all such Cases the Votes of both Houses shall be determined by yeas and Nays, and the Names of the Persons voting for and against the Bill shall be entered on the Journal of each House respectively. If any Bill shall not be returned by the President within ten Days (Sundays excepted) after it shall have been presented to him, the Same shall be a Law, in like Manner as if he had signed it, unless the Congress by their Adjournment prevent its Return, in which Case it shall not be a Law.

Every Order, Resolution, or Vote to which the Concurrence of the Senate and House of Representatives may be necessary (except on a question of Adjournment) shall be presented to the President of the United States; and before the Same shall take Effect, shall be approved by him, or being disapproved by him, shall be repassed by two thirds of the Senate and House of Representatives, according to the Rules and Limitations prescribed in the Case of a Bill.

Section. 8. The Congress shall have Power To lay and collect Taxes, Duties, Imposts and Excises, to pay the Debts and provide for the common Defence and general Welfare of the United States; but all Duties, Imposts and Excises shall be uniform throughout the United States;

To borrow Money on the credit of the United States;
To regulate Commerce with foreign Nations, and among the several States, and with the Indian Tribes;
To establish an uniform Rule of Naturalization, and uniform Laws on the subject of Bankruptcies throughout the United States;
To coin Money, regulate the Value thereof, and of foreign Coin, and fix the Standard of Weights and Measures;
To provide for the Punishment of counterfeiting the Securities and current Coin of the United States;
To establish Post Offices and post Roads;
To promote the Progress of Science and useful Arts, by securing for limited Times to Authors and Inventors the exclusive Right to their respective Writings and Discoveries;
To constitute Tribunals inferior to the supreme Court;
To define and punish Piracies and Felonies committed on the high Seas, and Offences against the Law of Nations;
To declare War, grant Letters of Marque and Reprisal, and make Rules concerning Captures on Land and Water;
To raise and support Armies, but no Appropriation of Money to that Use shall be for a longer Term than two Years;
To provide and maintain a Navy;
To make Rules for the Government and Regulation of the land and naval Forces;
To provide for calling forth the Militia to execute the Laws of the Union, suppress Insurrections and repel Invasions;
To provide for organizing, arming, and disciplining, the Militia, and for governing such Part of them as may be employed in the Service of the United States, reserving to the States respectively, the Appointment of the Officers, and the Authority of training the Militia according to the discipline pre scribed by Congress;
To exercise exclusive Legislation in all Cases whatsoever, over such District (not exceeding ten Miles square) as may, by Cession of particular States, and the Acceptance of Congress, become the Seat of the Government of the United States, and to exercise like Authority over all Places purchased by the Consent of the Legislature of the State in which the Same shall be, for the Erection of Forts, Magazines, Arsenals, dock-Yards, and other needful Buildings;--And
To make all Laws which shall be necessary and proper for carrying into Execution the foregoing Powers, and all other Powers vested by this Constitution in the Government of the United States, or in any Department or Officer thereof.

Section. 9. The Migration or Importation of such Persons as any of the States now existing shall think proper to admit, shall not be prohibited by the Congress prior to the Year one thousand eight hundred and eight, but a Tax or duty may be imposed on such Importation, not exceeding ten dollars for each Person.
The Privilege of the Writ of Habeas Corpus shall not be suspended, unless when in Cases of Rebellion or Invasion the public Safety may require it.
No Bill of Attainder or ex post facto Law shall be passed.
No Capitation, or other direct, Tax shall be laid, unless in Proportion to the Census or enumeration herein before directed to be taken.
No Tax or Duty shall be laid on Articles exported from any State.
No Preference shall be given by any Regulation of Commerce or Revenue to the Ports of one State over those of another; nor shall Vessels bound to, or from, one State, be obliged to enter, clear, or pay Duties in `aanother.
No Money shall be drawn from the Treasury, but in Consequence of Appropriations made by Law; and a regular Statement and Account of the Receipts and Expenditures of all public Money shall be published from time to time.
No Title of Nobility shall be granted by the United States: And no Person holding any Office of Profit or Trust under them, shall, without the Consent of the Congress, accept of any present, Emolument,

Office, or Title, of any kind what ever, from any King, Prince, or foreign State.

Section. 10. No State shall enter into any Treaty, Alliance, or Confederation; grant Letters of Marque and Reprisal; coin Money; emit Bills of Credit; make any Thing but gold and silver Coin a Tender in Payment of Debts; pass any Bill of Attainder, ex post facto Law, or Law impairing the Obligation of Contracts, or grant any Title of Nobility.

No State shall, without the Consent of the Congress, lay any Imposts or Duties on Imports or Exports, except what may be absolutely necessary for executing it's inspection Laws: and the net Produce of all Duties and Imposts, laid by any State on Imports or Exports, shall be for the Use of the

Treasury of the United States; and all such Laws shall be subject to the Revision and Controul of the Congress.

No State shall, without the Consent of Congress, lay any Duty of Tonnage, keep Troops, or Ships of War in time of Peace, enter into any Agreement or Compact with another State, or with a foreign Power, or engage in War, unless actually invaded, or in such imminent Danger as will not admit of delay.

Article. II.

Section. 1. The executive Power shall be vested in a President of the United States of America. He shall hold his Office during the Term of four Years, and, together with the Vice President, chosen for the same Term, be elected, as follows:

Each State shall appoint, in such Manner as the Legislature thereof may direct, a Number of Electors, equal to the whole Number of Senators and Representatives to which the State may be entitled in the Congress: but no Senator or Representative, or Person holding an Office of Trust or Profit under the United States, shall be appointed an Elector.

The Electors shall meet in their respective States, and vote by Ballot for two Persons, of whom one at least shall not be an Inhabitant of the same State with themselves. And they shall make a List of all the Persons voted for, and of the Number of Votes for each; which List they shall sign and certify, and transmit sealed to the Seat of the Government of the United States, directed to the President of the Senate. The President of the Senate shall, in the Presence of the Senate and House of Representatives, open all the Certificates, and the Votes shall then be counted. The Person having the greatest Number of Votes shall be the President, if such Number be a Majority of the whole Number of Electors appointed; and if there be more than one who have such Majority, and have an equal Number of Votes, then the House of Representatives shall immediately chuse by Ballot one of them for President; and if no Person have a Majority, then from the five highest on the List the said House shall in like Manner chuse the President. But in chusing the President, the Votes shall be taken by States, the representation from each State having one Vote; A quorum for this purpose shall consist of a Member or Members from two thirds of the States, and a Majority of all the States shall be necessary to a Choice. In every Case, after the Choice of the President, the Person having the greatest Number of Votes of the Electors shall be the Vice President. But if there should remain two or more who have equal Votes, the Senate shall chuse from them by Ballot the Vice President.

The Congress may determine the Time of chusing the Electors, and the Day on which they shall give their Votes; which Day shall be the same throughout the United States.

No Person except a natural born Citizen, or a Citizen of the United States, at the time of the Adoption of this Constitution, shall be eligible to the Office of President; neither shall any Person be eligible to that Office who shall not have attained to the Age of thirty five Years, and been fourteen Years a Resident within the United States.

In Case of the Removal of the President from Office, or of his Death, Resignation, or Inability to discharge the Powers and Duties of the said Office, the Same shall devolve on the Vice President, and the Congress may by Law provide for the Case of Removal, Death, Resignation or Inability, both of the President and Vice President, declaring what Officer shall then act as President, and such Officer shall act accordingly, until the Disability be removed, or a President shall be elected.

The President shall, at stated Times, receive for his Services, a Compensation, which shall neither be increased nor diminished during the Period for which he shall have been elected, and he shall not receive within that Period any other Emolument from the United States, or any of them.

Before he enter on the Execution of his Office, he shall take the following Oath or Affirmation:--"I do solemnly swear (or affirm) that I will faithfully execute the Office of President of the United States, and will to the best of my Ability, preserve, protect and defend the Constitution of the United States."

Section. 2. The President shall be Commander in Chief of the Army and Navy of the United States, and of the Militia of the several States, when called into the actual Service of the United States; he may require the Opinion, in writing, of the principal Officer in each of the executive Departments, upon any Subject relating to the Duties of their respective Offices, and he shall have Power to grant Reprieves and Pardons for Offences against the United States, except in Cases of Impeachment.

He shall have Power, by and with the Advice and Consent of the Senate, to make Treaties, provided two thirds of the Senators present concur; and he shall nominate, and by and with the Advice and Consent of the Senate, shall appoint Ambassadors, other public Ministers and Consuls, Judges of the supreme Court, and all other Officers of the United States, whose Appointments are not herein otherwise provided for, and which shall be established by Law: but the Congress may by Law vest the Appointment of such inferior Officers, as they think proper, in the President alone, in the Courts of Law, or in the Heads of Departments.

The President shall have Power to fill up all Vacancies that may happen during the Recess of the Senate, by granting Commissions which shall expire at the End of their next Session.

Section. 3. He shall from time to time give to the Congress Information of the State of the Union, and recommend to their Consideration such Measures as he shall judge necessary and expedient; he may, on extraordinary Occasions, convene both Houses, or either of them, and in Case of Disagreement between them, with Respect to the Time of Adjournment, he may adjourn them to such Time as he shall think proper; he shall receive Ambassadors and other public Ministers; he shall take Care that the Laws be faithfully executed, and shall Commission all the Officers of the United States.

Section. 4. The President, Vice President and all civil Officers of the United States, shall be removed from Office on Impeachment for, and Conviction of, Treason, Bribery, or other high Crimes and Misdemeanors.

Article III.

Section. 1. The judicial Power of the United States shall be vested in one supreme Court, and in such inferior Courts as the Congress may from time to time ordain and establish. The Judges, both of the supreme and inferior Courts, shall hold their Offices during good Behaviour, and shall, at stated Times, receive for their Services a Compensation, which shall not be diminished during their Continuance in Office.

Section. 2. The judicial Power shall extend to all Cases, in Law and Equity, arising under this Constitution, the Laws of the United States, and Treaties made, or which shall be made, under their Authority;--to all Cases affecting Ambassadors, other public Ministers and Consuls;--to all Cases of admiralty and maritime Jurisdiction;--to Controversies to which the United States shall be a Party;--to Controversies between two or more States;-- between a State and Citizens of another State;--between Citizens of different States;--between Citizens of the same State claiming Lands under Grants of different States, and between a State, or the Citizens thereof, and foreign States, Citizens or Subjects.

In all Cases affecting Ambassadors, other public Ministers and Consuls, and those in which a State shall be Party, the supreme Court shall have original Jurisdiction. In all the other Cases before mentioned, the supreme Court shall have appellate Jurisdiction, both as to Law and Fact, with such Exceptions, and under such Regulations as the Congress shall make.

The Trial of all Crimes, except in Cases of Impeachment, shall be by Jury; and such Trial shall be held in the State where the said Crimes shall have been committed; but when not committed within any State, the Trial shall be at such Place or Places as the Congress may by Law have directed.

Section. 3. Treason against the United States, shall consist only in levying War against them, or in adhering to their Enemies, giving them Aid and Comfort. No Person shall be convicted of Treason unless on the Testimony of two Witnesses to the same overt Act, or on Confession in open Court.

The Congress shall have Power to declare the Punishment of Treason, but no Attainder of Treason shall work Corruption of Blood, or Forfeiture except during the Life of the Person attainted.

Article. IV.

Section. 1. Full Faith and Credit shall be given in each State to the public Acts, Records, and judicial Proceedings of every other State. And the Congress may by general Laws prescribe the Manner in which such Acts, Records and Proceedings shall be proved, and the Effect thereof.

Section. 2. The Citizens of each State shall be entitled to all Privileges and Immunities of Citizens in the several States.

A Person charged in any State with Treason, Felony, or other Crime, who shall flee from Justice, and be found in another State, shall on Demand of the executive Authority of the State from which he fled, be delivered up, to be removed to the State having Jurisdiction of the Crime.

No Person held to Service or Labour in one State, under the Laws thereof, escaping into another, shall, in Consequence of any Law or Regulation therein, be discharged from such Service or Labour, but shall be delivered up on Claim of the Party to whom such Service or Labour may be due.

Section. 3. New States may be admitted by the Congress into this Union; but no new State shall be formed or erected within the Jurisdiction of any other State; nor any State be formed by the Junction of two or more States, or Parts of States, without the Consent of the Legislatures of the States concerned as well as of the Congress.

The Congress shall have Power to dispose of and make all needful Rules and Regulations respecting the Territory or other Property belonging to the United States; and nothing in this Constitution shall be so construed as to Prejudice any Claims of the United States, or of any particular State.

Section. 4. The United States shall guarantee to every State in this Union a Republican Form of Government, and shall protect each of them against Invasion; and on Application of the Legislature, or if the Executive (when the Legislature cannot be convened), against domestic Violence.

Article. V.

The Congress, whenever two thirds of both Houses shall deem it necessary, shall propose Amendments to this Constitution, or, on the Application of the Legislatures of two thirds of the several States, shall call a Convention for proposing Amendments, which, in either Case, shall be valid to all

Intents and Purposes, as Part of this Constitution, when ratified by the Legislatures of three fourths of the several States, or by Conventions in three fourths thereof, as the one or the other Mode of Ratification may be proposed by the Congress; Provided that no Amendment which may be made prior to the Year One thousand eight hundred and eight shall in any Manner affect the first and fourth Clauses in the Ninth Section of the first Article; and that no State, without its Consent, shall be deprived of its equal Suffrage in the Senate.

Article. VI.

All Debts contracted and Engagements entered into, before the Adoption of this Constitution, shall be as valid against the United States under this Constitution, as under the Confederation.

This Constitution, and the Laws of the United States which shall be made in Pursuance thereof; and all Treaties made, or which shall be made, under the Authority of the United States, shall be the supreme Law of the Land; and the Judges in every State shall be bound thereby, any Thing in the Constitution or Laws of any State to the Contrary notwithstanding.

The Senators and Representatives before mentioned, and the Members of the several State Legislatures, and all executive and judicial Officers, both of the United States and of the several States, shall be bound by Oath or Affirmation, to support this Constitution; but no religious Test shall ever be required as a Qualification to any Office or public Trust under the United States.

Article. VII.

The Ratification of the Conventions of nine States, shall be sufficient for the Establishment of this Constitution between the States so ratifying the Same.

Done in Convention by the Unanimous Consent of the States present the Seventeenth Day of September in the Year of our Lord one thousand seven hundred and Eighty seven and of the independence of the United States of America the Twelfth In witness whereof We have hereunto subscribed our Names, (*Signed by George Washington, President and all attending members.*)

BILL OF RIGHTS

Congress of the United States

begun and held at the City of New York, on

Wednesday the fourth of March, one thousand seven hundred and eighty nine.

THE Conventions of a number of the States, having at the time of their adopting the Constitution, expressed a desire, in order to prevent misconstruction or abuse of its powers, that further declaratory and restrictive clauses should be added: And as extending the ground of public confidence in the Government, will best ensure the beneficent ends of its institution.

RESOLVED by the Senate and House of Representatives of the United States of America, in Congress assembled, two thirds of both Houses concurring, that the following Articles be proposed to the Legislatures of the several States, as amendments to the Constitution of the United States, all, or any of which Articles, when ratified by three fourths of the said Legislatures, to be valid to all intents and purposes, as part of the said Constitution; viz.

ARTICLES in addition to, and Amendment of the Constitution of the United States of America, proposed by Congress, and ratified by the Legislatures of the several States, pursuant to the fifth Article of the original Constitution

Article I

After the first enumeration required by the first article of the Constitution, there shall be one representative for every thirty thousand, until the number shall amount to one hundred, after which the proportion shall be so regulated by Congress, that there shall be not less than one hundred representatives, nor less than one representative for every forty thousand persons, until the number of representatives shall amount to two hundred; after which the proportion shall be so regulated by Congress, that there shall be not less than two hundred representatives, nor more than one representative for every fifty thousand persons.

Article II

No law varying the compensation for the services of the Senators and Representatives, shall take effect, until an election of Representatives shall have intervened.

Article III

Congress shall make no law respecting an establishment of religion, or prohibiting the free exercise thereof; or abridging the freedom of speech, or of the press; or the right of the people peaceably to assemble, and to petition the Government for a redress of grievances.

Article IV

A well regulated Militia, being necessary to the security of a free State, the right of the people to keep and bear Arms, shall not be infringed.

Article V

No Soldier shall, in time of peace be quartered in any house, without the consent of the Owner, nor in time of war, but in a manner to be prescribed by law.

Article VI

The right of the people to be secure in their persons, houses, papers, and effects, against unreasonable searches and seizures, shall not be violated, and no Warrants shall issue, but upon probable cause, supported by Oath or affirmation, and particularly describing the place to be searched, and the persons or things to be seized.

Article VII

No person shall be held to answer for a capital, or otherwise infamous crime, unless on a presentment or indictment of a Grand Jury, except in cases arising in the land or naval forces, or in the Militia, when in actual service in time of War or public danger; nor shall any person be subject for the same offence to be twice put in jeopardy of life or limb; nor shall be compelled in any criminal case to be a witness against himself, nor be deprived of life, liberty, or property, without due process of law; nor shall private property be taken for public use, without just compensation.

Article VIII

In all criminal prosecutions, the accused shall enjoy the right to a speedy and public trial, by an impartial jury of the State and district wherein the crime shall have been committed, which district shall have been previously ascertained by law, and to be informed of the nature and cause of the accusation; to be confronted with the witnesses against him; to have compulsory process for obtaining witnesses in his favor, and to have the Assistance of Counsel for his defence.

Article IX

In Suits at common law, where the value in controversy shall exceed twenty dollars, the right of trial by jury shall be preserved, and no fact tried by a jury, shall be otherwise re-examined in any Court of the United States, than according to the rules of the common law.

Article X

Excessive bail shall not be required, nor excessive fines imposed, nor cruel and unusual punishments inflicted.

Article XI

The enumeration in the Constitution, of certain rights, shall not be construed to deny or disparage others retained by the people.

Article XII

The powers not delegated to the United States by the Constitution, nor prohibited by it to the States, are reserved to the States respectively, or to the people.

The Monroe Doctrine

December 2, 1823

FELLOW CITIZENS of the Senate and House of Representatives. . . At the proposal of the Russian Imperial Government, made through the minister of the Emperor residing here, a full power and instructions have been transmitted to the minister of the United States at St. Petersburg to arrange by amicable negotiation the respective rights and interests of the two nations on the northwest coast of this continent. A similar proposal has been made by His Imperial Majesty to the Government of Great Britain, which has likewise been acceded to. The Government of the United States has been desirous by this friendly proceeding of manifesting the great value which they have invariably attached to the friendship of the Emperor and their solicitude to cultivate the best understanding with his Government. In the discussions to which this interest has given rise and in the arrangements by which they may terminate the occasion has been judged proper for asserting, as a principle in which the rights and interests of the United States are involved, that the American continents, by the free and independent condition which they have assumed and maintain, are henceforth not to be considered as subjects for future colonization by any European powers. . .

It was stated at the commencement of the last session that a great effort was then making in Spain and Portugal to improve the condition of the people of those countries, and that it appeared to be conducted with extraordinary moderation. It need scarcely be remarked that the results have been so far very different from what was then anticipated.

Of events in that quarter of the globe, with which we have so much intercourse and from which we derive our origin, we have always been anxious and interested spectators. The citizens of the United States cherish sentiments the most friendly in favor of the liberty and happiness of their fellow-men on that side of the Atlantic. In the wars of the European powers in matters relating to themselves we have never taken any part, nor does it comport with our policy to do so. It is only when our rights are invaded or seriously menaced that we resent injuries or make preparation for our defense.

With the movements in this hemisphere we are of necessity more immediately connected, and by causes which must be obvious to all enlightened and impartial observers. The political system of the allied powers is essentially different in this respect from that of America. This difference proceeds from that which exists in their respective Governments; and to the defense of our own, which has been achieved by the loss of so much blood and treasure, and matured by the wisdom of their most enlightened citizens, and under which we have enjoyed unexampled felicity, this whole nation is devoted.

We owe it, therefore, to candor and to the amicable relations existing between the United States and those powers to declare that we should consider any attempt on their part to extend their system to any portion of this hemisphere as dangerous to our peace and safety. With the existing colonies or dependencies of any European power we have not interfered and shall not interfere. But with the Governments who have declared their independence and maintain it, and whose independence we have, on great consideration and on just principles, acknowledged, we could not view any interposition for the purpose of oppressing them, or controlling in any other manner their destiny, by any European power in any other light than as the manifestation of an unfriendly disposition toward the United States. In the war between those new Governments and Spain we declared our neutrality at the time of their recognition, and to this we have adhered, and shall continue to adhere, provided no change shall occur which, in the judgement of the competent authorities of this Government, shall make a corresponding change on the part of the United States indispensable to their security.

The late events in Spain and Portugal shew that Europe is still unsettled. Of this important fact no stronger proof can be adduced than that the allied powers should have thought it proper, on any principle satisfactory to themselves, to have interposed by force in the internal concerns of Spain. To what extent such interposition may be carried, on the same principle, is a question in which all independent powers whose governments differ from theirs are interested, even those most remote, and surely none of them more so than the United States. Our policy in regard to Europe, which was adopted at an early stage of the wars which have so long agitated that quarter of the globe, nevertheless remains the same, which is, not to interfere in the internal concerns of any of its powers; to consider the government de facto as the legitimate government for us; to cultivate friendly relations with it, and to preserve those relations by a frank, firm, and manly policy, meeting in all instances the just claims of every power, submitting to injuries from none.

But in regard to those continents circumstances are eminently and conspicuously different. It is impossible that the allied powers should extend their political system to any portion of either continent without endangering our peace and happiness; nor can anyone believe that our southern brethren, if left to themselves, would adopt it of their own accord. It is equally impossible, therefore, that we should behold such interposition in any form with indifference. If we look to the comparative strength and resources of Spain and those new Governments, and their distance from each other, it must be obvious that she can never subdue them. It is still the true policy of the United States to leave the parties to themselves, in hope that other powers will pursue the same course. . . .

Allan Pinkerton of the secret service, President Lincoln, and Major General John McClernand, 1862.

The Gettysburg Address

November 19, 1863

Four score and seven years ago our fathers brought forth on this continent a new nation, conceived in liberty and dedicated to the proposition that all men are created equal.

Now we are engaged in a great civil war, testing whether that nation or any nation so conceived and so dedicated can long endure. We are met on a great battlefield of that war. We have come to dedicate a portion of that field as a final resting-place for those who here gave their lives that that nation might live. It is altogether fitting and proper that we should do this.

But in a larger sense, we cannot dedicate, we cannot consecrate, we cannot hallow this ground. The brave men, living and dead who struggled here have consecrated it far above our poor power to add or detract. The world will little note nor long remember what we say here, but it can never forget what they did here. It is for us the living rather to be dedicated here to the unfinished work which they who fought here have thus far so nobly advanced. It is rather for us to be here dedicated to the great task remaining before us --that from these honored dead we take increased devotion to that cause for which they gave the last full measure of devotion-- that we here highly resolve that these dead shall not have died in vain, that this nation under God shall have a new birth of freedom, and that government of the people, by the people, for the people shall not perish from the earth.

"The Star Spangled Banner"

It was the valiant defense of Fort McHenry by American forces during the British attack on September 13, 1814 that inspired 35-year old, poet-lawyer Francis Scott Key to write the poem which was to become our national anthem, "The Star-Spangled Banner." The poem was written to match the meter of the English song, "To Anacreon in Heaven." In 1931 the Congress of The United States of America enacted legislation that made "The Star-Spangled Banner" the official national anthem.

Oh, say can you see, by the dawn's early light,
What so proudly we hailed at the twilight's last gleaming?
Whose broad stripes and bright stars, through the perilous fight,
O'er the ramparts we watched, were so gallantly streaming?
And the rockets' red glare, the bombs bursting in air,
Gave proof through the night that our flag was still there.
O say, does that star-spangled banner yet wave
O'er the land of the free and the home of the brave?

On the shore, dimly seen through the mists of the deep,
Where the foe's haughty host in dread silence reposes,
What is that which the breeze, o'er the towering steep,
As it fitfully blows, now conceals, now discloses?
Now it catches the gleam of the morning's first beam,
In full glory reflected now shines on the stream:
'Tis the star-spangled banner! O long may it wave
O'er the land of the free and the home of the brave.

And where is that band who so vauntingly swore
That the havoc of war and the battle's confusion
A home and a country should leave us no more?
Their blood has wiped out their foul footstep's pollution.
No refuge could save the hireling and slave
From the terror of flight, or the gloom of the grave:
And the star-spangled banner in triumph doth wave
O'er the land of the free and the home of the brave.

Oh! thus be it ever, when freemen shall stand
Between their loved homes and the war's desolation!
Blest with victory and peace, may the heaven-rescued land
Praise the Power that hath made and preserved us a nation.
Then conquer we must, when our cause it is just,
And this be our motto: "In God is our trust."
And the star-spangled banner in triumph shall wave
O'er the land of the free and the home of the brave!

"Then, in that hour of deliverance, my heart spoke. Does not such a country, and such defenders of their country, deserve a song?..."

FRANCIS SCOTT KEY
(1779 - 1843)

Oh say, can you see by the dawn's early light,
What so proudly we hail'd at the twilight's last gleaming,
Whose broad stripes and bright stars, through the clouds of the fight,
O'er the ramparts we watch'd were so gallantly streaming?
And the rocket's red glare — the bomb bursting in air
Gave proof through the night that our flag was still there
Oh say, does that star-spangled banner yet wave
O'er the land of the free and the home of the brave?

On the shore dimly seen through the mists of the deep,
Where the foe's haughty host in dread silence reposes,
What is that which the breeze, o'er the towering steep,
As it fitfully blows, half conceals, half discloses?
Now it catches the gleam of the morning's first beam,
In full glory reflected, now shines on the stream,
'Tis the star-spangled banner — Oh long may it wave
O'er the land of the free & the home of the brave.

And where is the host that so vauntingly swore
That the havoc of war & the battle's confusion
A home and a country should leave us no more?
Their blood has wash'd out their foul footsteps' pollution.
No refuge could save the hireling & slave
From the terror of flight or the gloom of the grave,
And the star-spangled banner in triumph doth wave
O'er the land of the free & the home of the brave.

O thus be it ever when freemen shall stand
Between their lov'd home and the war's desolation;
Blest with vict'ry & peace may the Heav'n-rescued land
Praise the Power that hath made & preserv'd us a nation!
Then conquer we must, when our cause it is just,
And this be our motto — "In God is our trust"
And the star-spangled banner in triumph shall wave
O'er the land of the free & the home of the brave.

Washington
Aug. 29 — 42

F. S. Key

Francis Scott Key was born on August 1, 1779 in Maryland. Although opposed to the war, he served for a brief period in the Georgetown Light Field Artillery.

In September 1814 Key sailed on a truce ship to negotiate the release of a friend, Dr. William Bean but, was detained with Bean by the British until after the attack on Baltimore.

Key's ship was 8 miles below Fort McHenry, Maryland during the bombardment, guarded by a British warship. He witnessed the attack on the Fort. The British were repelled. Inspired by the sight of our flag proudly flying over the Fort. Keys wrote the words to our national anthem "The Star Spangled Banner."

Today, the flag he so honored flies day and night at Fort McHenry a reminder of those events in 1814.

"Star-Spangled Banner"

This was the actual flag flying above Fort McHenry at Baltimore when the British attacked it on September 13, 1814. Francis Scott Key had gone aboard a British ship seeking the release of a friend. He was detained throughout the night. The sight of the American flag still flying over the fortress the next morning inspired Key to write what, in 1931, became our National Anthem. The original Ft. McHenry flag is displayed in the Smithsonian institution in Washington. Its design, born with the second flag act on January 13, 1794, is the only one ever to have more than thirteen stripes.

Betsy Ross

In June 1776, brave Betsy was a widow struggling to run her own upholstery business. Upholsterers in colonial America not only worked on furniture but did all manner of sewing work, which for some included making flags. According to Betsy, General Washington showed her a rough design of the flag that included a six-pointed star. Betsy, a standout with the scissors, demonstrated how to cut a five-pointed star in a single snip. Impressed, the committee entrusted Betsy with making our first flag.

The Grand Union Flag - 1776

The first national flag authorized by the Continental Congress. The thirteen alternating stripes represent the colonies and the crosses symbolize the hope of remaining attached to Britain.

United States Flag - 1776

In May 1776 Betsy Ross a seamstress, was chosen by a Congressional Committee led by General George Washington to make the first Stars and Stripes. The 13 stars in a circle on a blue field represented a "Union without end" and the 13 stripes for the original colonies. On July 4th 1776 the Continental Congress declared the United States to be independent of Great Britain. In June 1777 the Stars and Stripes was declared our official flag.

United States Flag - 1795

By 1792 Vermont and Kentucky joined the Union. Now there were fifteen states. Congress declared on January 15, 1794 that " From and after the first day of May 1795, the flag of the United States be 15 stripes and the Union be 15 stars. The circular format, was abandoned after being in use for 18 years.

United States Flag - Today

Fifty stars grace our flag since 1960, with the admission of Hawaii as a state of the Union. In less than two hundred years The American Union has prospered and grown from a small group of colonies along the Atlantic seacoast to its present wealth, power and size. Fifty states extending from ocean to ocean and beyond.

"The Spirit of 76"

By Archibald M. Willard

Originally entitled "Yankee Doodle", the painting "Spirit of `76" captures the spirit of the indomitable early American Patriots of 1776. The "Spirit Of '76" is one of the most widely recognized images in the world. Archibald M. Willard did the 8' x 10' oil painting around 1875. It depicts an adult drummer, drummer boy, and fifer marching across a battlefield during the American Revolution.

John Paul Jones

After conducting sea raids on the coast of Britain, he took command in 1779 of a rebuilt French merchant ship, renamed the U.S.S. Bonhomme Richard to honor Benjamin Franklin. On September 23, 1779, Jones engaged the British frigate Serapis in the North Sea, daring to sail in close, lashing his vessel to the British ship, and fighting the battle at point-blank range. During the fight two of his cannon burst, and the British captain asked Jones if he was ready to surrender. Replied Jones; "Sir, I have not yet begun to fight." The American crew finally boarded the Serapis after the British had struck her colors, and from the deck of the Serapis they watched the U.S.S. Bonhomme Richard sink into the North Sea.

The U.S.S. Constitution

Nicknamed "Old Ironsides" because bullets could not penetrate her tough oak sides. One of the first of the original six frigates that made up the U.S. Navy. A 44-gun frigate she carried a crew of more than 450. The ship served in the undeclared naval war with France (1798-1800). Was the Flagship in the Mediterranean squadron in the Tripolitan War (1801-05). In the War of 1812 the Constitution won battles with the British frigates Guerriere and Java. Its last combat tour in 1814-15.

Scheduled to be scrapped in 1830, Oliver Wendell Holmes's poem "Old Ironsides" inspired a public movement to save it. Restored in 1925, the Constitution is now The oldest commissioned vessel in the US Navy. At Present she serves as a museum ship moored in Boston harbor.

The Liberty Bell

A chime that changed the world occurred on July 8, 1776, when the Liberty Bell rang out from the tower of Independence Hall summoning citizens to hear the first public reading of the Declaration of Independence by Colonel John Nixon. The Pennsylvania Assembly ordered the Bell in 1751 to commemorate the 50-year anniversary of William Penn's 1701 Charter of Privileges.

Paul Revere

"Silversmith and Patriot"

Paul Revere was the Patriot' s most trusted messenger. A network to watch the movements of the British Redcoats was set up. A signal was to come from the steeple of North Church. The signals were one lantern if by land and two if by sea. On April 18, 1775, two lanterns were hung to signal that the British were coming to Lexington and Concord by sea. Revere was waiting for the signal. When he saw the lanterns he rowed across the Charles River to Charlestown, mounted a horse and started his famous ride to Lexington at about 11 PM. Revere rode through the towns to Lexington and on toward Concord warning all along the way that "The Regulars were coming".

Benjamin Franklin

Inventor, writer, printer, publisher, diplomat, statesman. Curious by nature, Franklin was self taught on many subjects. Much of what he learned would come in handy later while serving in the Second Continental Congress. He served on committees that drafted the Declaration of Independence, handled secret correspondence, and secretly obtained military supplies for the Revolution. The amazing Franklin experimented with electricity and invented the Franklin Stove. His many published works included "The Pennsylvania Gazette", and "Poor Richard's Almanac". It would be impossible to list all his accomplishments here.

Dolley Madison

For half a century she was the most important woman in the social circles of America. Dolley made her home the center of society when her husband James Madison began, in 1801, his eight years as Thomas Jefferson's Secretary of State. She assisted at the White House when President Jefferson, a bachelor, asked her to serve as his hostess at public functions. She presided at the first inaugural ball in Washington when her husband became Chief Executive in 1809. To this day she remains one of the best known and best loved ladies of the White House.

Katherine Lee Bates

"America The Beautiful" was written by Katharine Lee Bates noted American poetess and English professor at Wellesley College. She wrote "America The Beautiful" in 1893 after a trip to Colorado Springs, Colorado. She was inspired by the majestic views from the summit of Pikes Peak overlooking Colorado Springs. It first appeared in print in "The Congregationalist" two years later, and within a few months Silas G. Pratt set the poem to music. In 1904, after many requests for use in publications and special services, Bates rewrote it to simplify the text. She made one additional change in the wording of the third stanza a few years later, to give us the version we know today.

America the Beautiful

by Katharine Lee Bates

O beautiful for spacious skies,
For amber waves of grain,
For purple mountain majesties
Above the fruited plain!
America! America!
God shed his grace on thee
And crown thy good with
brotherhood
From sea to shining sea!

O beautiful for pilgrim feet
Whose stern impassioned - stress
A thoroughfare for freedom beat
Across the wilderness!
America! America!
God mend thine every flaw,
Confirm thy soul in self-control,
Thy liberty in law!

O beautiful for heroes proved In
liberating strife.
Who more than self the country
loved And mercy more than life!
America! America!
May God thy gold refine
Till all success be nobleness
And every gain divine!

O beautiful for patriot dream
That sees beyond the years
Thine alabaster cities gleam
Undimmed by human tears!
America! America!
God shed his grace on thee
And crown thy good with
brotherhood
From sea to shining sea!

O beautiful for halcyon skies,
For amber waves of grain,
For purple mountain majesties
Above the enameled plain!
America! America!
God shed his grace on thee
Till souls wax fair as earth and air
And music-hearted sea!

O beautiful for pilgrims feet,
Whose stern impassioned stress
A thoroughfare for freedom beat
Across the wilderness!
America ! America !
God shed his grace on thee
Till paths be wrought through
wilds of thought By pilgrim
foot and knee!

O beautiful for glory-tale
Of liberating strife
When once and twice,
for man's avail
Men lavished precious life!
America! America!
God shed his grace on thee
Till selfish gain no longer
stain The banner of the free!

O beautiful for patriot dream
That sees beyond the years
Thine alabaster cities gleam
Undimmed by human tears!
America! America!
God shed his grace on thee
Till nobler men keep once
again Thy whiter jubilee!

“America”

(“My Country Tis OF Thee”)

By Samuel Francis Smith

My country tis of thee,
Sweet land of liberty,
Of thee I sing.

Land where my fathers died!
Land of the Pilgrim's pride!
From every mountain side,
Let freedom ring!

My native country, thee,
Land of the noble free,
Thy name I love.
I love thy rocks and rills,
Thy woods and templed hills;
My heart with rapture fills
Like that above.

Let music swell the breeze,
And ring from all the trees
Sweet freedom's song.
Let mortal tongues awake;
Let all that breathe partake;
Let rocks their silence break,
The sound prolong.

Our father's God to, Thee,
Author of liberty,
To Thee we sing.
Long may our land be bright
With freedom's holy light;
Protect us by Thy might,
Great God, our King!

Samuel Francis Smith

American Baptist clergyman and poet. He is remembered as the author of the national hymn "America", written while he was a student at Andover Theological Seminary.

While Smith was a seminary student he accepted literary work to support himself. In 1832 during his last year musician Lowell Mason asked Smith to translate some German verses for a song book he was preparing. One the tunes he handed Smith was a German patriotic hymn, "God Bless Our Native Land." When Smith read it, he felt that the United states needed a stirring national poem too. Writing on scraps of paper, he finished a poem he titled "America" within thirty minutes. Set to the tune for “God Save the Queen” the song gained immediate popularity.

"Uncle Sam"

By James Montgomery Flagg

Originally published as the cover for the July 6, 1916, issue of Leslie's Weekly with the title "What Are You Doing for Preparedness?" this portrait of "Uncle Sam" went on to become-according to its creator, James Montgomery Flagg-"the most famous poster in the world." Over four million copies were printed between 1917 and 1918, as United States entered World War I and began sending troops and materiel into war zones.

Flagg (1877-1960) contributed forty-six works to support the war effort. He was a member of the first Civilian Preparedness Committee organized in New York in 1917. He also served as a member of Charles Dana Gibson's Committee of Pictorial Publicity, which was organized under the federal government's Committee on Public Information.

Because of its overwhelming popularity, the image was later adapted for use in World War II. Upon presenting President Franklin Delano Roosevelt a copy of the poster, Flagg remarked that he had been his own model for Uncle Sam to save the modeling fee. Roosevelt was impressed and replied: "I congratulate you on your resourcefulness in saving model hire. Your method suggests Yankee forebears."

Uncle Sam is one of the most popular personifications of the United States. However, the term "Uncle Sam" is of somewhat obscure derivation. Historical sources attribute the name to a meat packer who supplied meat to the army during the War of 1812, Samuel (Uncle Sam) Wilson. "Uncle Sam" Wilson was a man of great fairness, reliability, and honesty, who was devoted to his country, qualities now associated with "our" Uncle Sam.

I WANT YOU
FOR U.S. ARMY
NEAREST RECRUITING STATION

"The only thing we have to fear is fear itself."

Franklin D. Roosevelt

Franklin Delano Roosevelt

1882 - 1945

32nd President

In the summer of 1921, when he was 39, Roosevelt was stricken with polio. Demonstrating indomitable courage, he fought to regain the use of his legs, particularly through swimming. He was elected Governor of New York in 1928.

Roosevelt was elected to the Presidency in November 1932 at the depth of the Great Depression. He helped the American people regain faith in themselves. He brought hope as he promised prompt, vigorous action. In his first "hundred days," he proposed, and Congress enacted, a sweeping program to bring recovery to business and agriculture. He established the Tennessee Valley Authority, which helped bring relief to the unemployed and to those in danger of losing farms and homes.

Roosevelt's "New Deal" program helped the Nation achieve some measure of recovery by 1935. Wanting to do more he reformed Social Security, increased taxes on the wealthy, put new controls over banks and public utilities, and established an enormous work relief program for the unemployed. Roosevelt was elected to four terms shattering the two term tradition, Since 1951 the office of President has been restricted to two terms.

Roosevelt tried to keep the United States out of the war in Europe, and yet strengthen nations threatened or attacked. When the Japanese attacked Pearl Harbor on December 7, 1941, he directed the organization of our Nation's manpower and resources as we entered World War II. As the war drew to a close in early 1945 he died of a cerebral hemorrhage.

"Ask not what your country can do for you--ask what you can do for your country."

John F. Kennedy

John F. Kennedy

1917 to 1963
35th President

On November 22, 1963, when he was hardly past his first thousand days in office, John Fitzgerald Kennedy was killed by an assassin's bullets as his motorcade wound through Dallas, Texas. Kennedy was the youngest man elected President; he was the youngest to die.

As President, he set out to redeem his campaign pledge to get America moving again. His economic programs launched the country on its longest sustained expansion since World War II; before his death, he laid plans for a massive assault on privation and poverty. He took vigorous action in the cause of equal rights, calling for new civil rights legislation. His vision of America extended to the quality of the national culture and the central role of the arts in a vital society. With the Alliance for Progress and the Peace Corps, he brought American idealism to the aid of developing nations.

Kennedy had major challenges from the Soviet Union including the building of the Berlin Wall. Later, when the Russians began to install nuclear missiles in Cuba. Kennedy quarantined all offensive weapons bound for Cuba. Faced with the threat of nuclear war, Russia backed down and took the missiles away. After the Cuban crisis, both sides had a vital interest in stopping the spread of nuclear weapons and slowing the arms race. This lead to the 1963 test ban treaty.

In May 1961, President John F. Kennedy announced that the United States would fly men to the Moon and back within the decade. Astronaut Alan B. Shepard Jr. became America's first man in space on May 5, 1961 with Shepard's 15-minute sub orbital flight in Freedom 7. On February 20, 1962, John Glenn became the first American to orbit the Earth. He piloted his Mercury-Atlas 6 "Friendship 7" spacecraft on a successful three-orbit mission around the Earth paving the way for space exploration as we know it today.

*"That's one small step for a man,
one giant leap for Mankind."*

Neil Armstrong

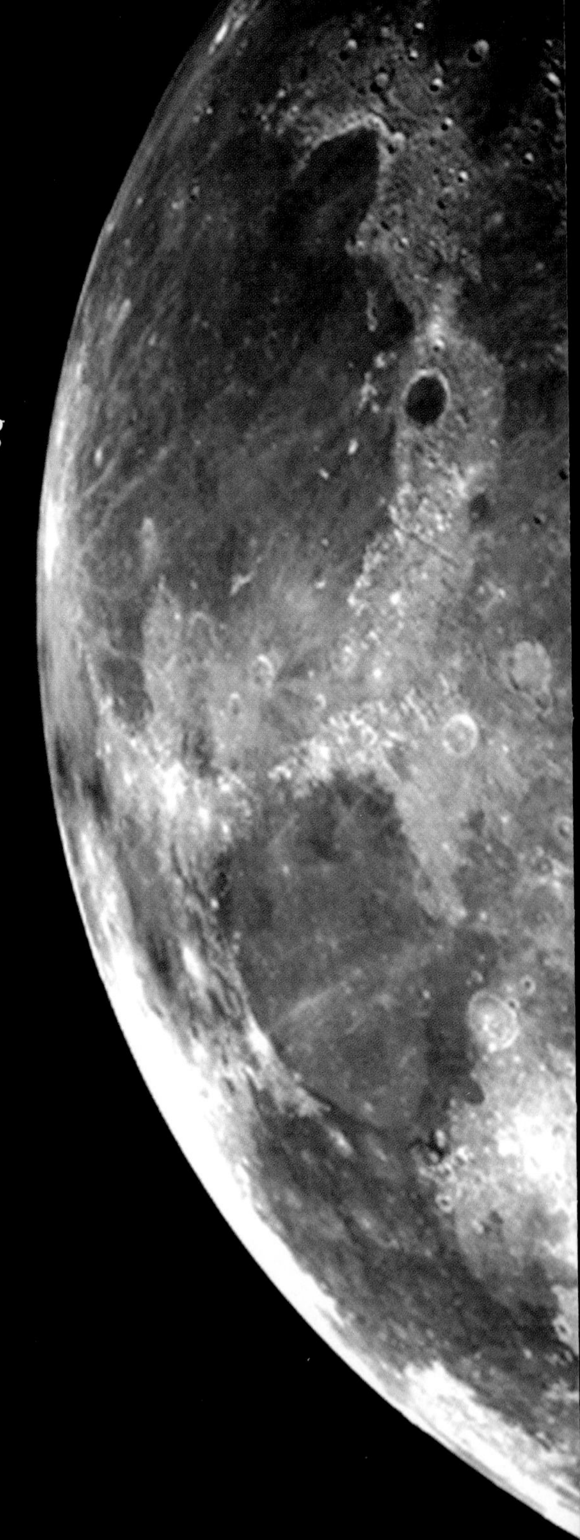

Neil Armstrong

Apollo 11 Astronaut

Neil A. Armstrong commanded the Gemini 8 mission and became the first human to walk on the moon as commander of Apollo XI. He was selected as an astronaut by NASA in 1962.

On July 16, 1969, Apollo 11 astronauts Armstrong, Buzz Aldrin, and Mike Collins departed for the moon. Four days later, Armstrong and Aldrin landed their Lunar Module in the moon's Sea of Tranquility. Armstrong, and then Aldrin, stepped onto the surface and became the first humans to leave their footprints in the lunar dust. They explored the surface and gathered moon rocks for over two hours. The next day they fired off the surface and rejoined Collins in the orbiting mother ship.

Armstrong left NASA in 1971 and became a professor of aeronautical engineering at the University of Cincinnati, where he taught until 1981. He has since been in the business world and he currently is chairman of CTA, Inc. Neil Armstrong was inducted into the Astronaut Hall of Fame on March 19, 1993.

"The Eagle has landed."

Neil Armstrong

Buzz Aldrin

Buzz Aldrin

Apollo 11 Astronaut

On October 1963, Buzz was selected by NASA as one of the early astronauts. In November 1966, he established a new record for Extra-Vehicular Activity in space on the Gemini 12 orbital flight mission.

As Backup Command Module Pilot for Apollo 8, man's first flight around the moon, he significantly improved operational techniques for astronautical navigation star display. Then, on July 20, 1969, Buzz and Neil Armstrong made their historic Apollo 11 moon walk, thus becoming the first two humans to set foot on another world. This unprecedented heroic endeavor was witnessed by the largest worldwide television audience in history.

Upon returning from the moon, Buzz embarked on an international goodwill tour. He was presented the Presidential Medal of Freedom, the highest honor amongst over 50 other distinguished awards and medals from the United States and numerous other countries.

The American Creed

I believe in the United States of America as a Government of the People, by the people, for the people; whose just powers are derived from the consent of the governed; a democracy in a republic; a sovereign Nation of many sovereign States; a perfect union, one and inseparable; established upon those principiles of freedom, equality, justice and humanity for which American patriots sacrificed their lives and fortunes.

I therefore believe it is my duty to my country to love it; to support its Constitution; to obey its laws; to respect its flag, and to defend it against all enemies.

"The American Creed" by William Tyler Written in 1917.
Accepted for the American People by the House of Representatives April 13, 1918.

George W. Bush

43rd President of the United States

"The American people will never forget
the cruelty that was done here and in
New York, and in the sky over Pennsylvania.
The entire nation shares in your sadness.
And we pray for you and your loved ones.

Comments By Mr. Red Skelton

Comedian and Great American

The following words were spoken by the late famous comedian Red Skelton on his television program as he related the story of his teacher, Mr. Laswell, who felt his students had come to think of the Pledge of Allegiance as merely something to recite in class each day. Now, more than ever, listen to the meaning of these words.

"I've been listening to you boys and girls recite the Pledge of Allegiance all semester and it seems as though it is becoming monotonous to you. If I may, may I recite it and try to explain to you the meaning of each word?"

I -- *me, an individual, a committee of one.*

Pledge -- *dedicate all of my worldly goods to give without self pity.*

Allegiance -- *my love and my devotion.*

To the flag -- *our standard, Old Glory, a symbol of freedom. Wherever she waves, there's respect because your loyalty has given her a dignity that shouts freedom is everybody's job!*

United -- *that means that we have all come together.*

States -- *individual communities that have united into 48 great states. Forty-eight individual communities with pride and dignity and purpose; all divided with imaginary boundaries, yet united to a common purpose, and that's love for country.*

And to the republic -- *a state in which sovereign power is invested in representatives chosen by the people to govern. And government is the people and it's from the people to the leaders, not from the leaders to the people.*

For which it stands, one nation -- *one nation, meaning "so blessed by God"*

Indivisible -- *incapable of being divided.*

With liberty -- *which is freedom -- the right of power to live one's own life without threats, fear or somesort of retaliation.*

And Justice -- *the principle or quality of dealing fairly with others.*

For all -- *which means, boys and girls, it's as much your country as it is mine.*

"Since I was a small boy, two states have been added to our country and two words have been added to the pledge of Allegiance... UNDER GOD Wouldn't it be a pity if someone said "that is a prayer", and that it would be eliminated from schools too?"

"God Bless America!"

The
Pledge of Allegiance

I Pledge allegiance
to the flag
of the
United States of America
and to the Republic
for which it stands,
one Nation under God,
indivisible,
with liberty and justice
for all.

The people of France gave the Statue to the people of the United States in recognition of the friendship established during the American Revolution. Over the years, the Statue of Liberty has grown to include freedom and democracy as well as this international friendship.

An American
I am Proud to be.
In a country that allows
all to be free.
We can come and go,
and do as we please.
Speak our minds, and
have freedom of choice.
Walk where we want
with whom we please.
The flag that we honor
blows softly in the breeze.
An American
I am proud to be.
To pledge allegiance to
my country tis of thee.
Sweet land of liberty.
An American
I am Proud to be.

Gerri L.Riley
3/19/82

Presidents Of  The United States

President	Party	Office Term
George Washington	Federalist	1789-1797
John Adams	Federalist	1797-1801
Thomas Jefferson	Republican	1801-1809
James Madison	Republican	1809-1817
James Monroe	Republican	1817-1825
John Quincy Adams	Republican	1825-1829
Andrew Jackson	Democratic	1829-1837
Martin Van Buren	Democratic	1837-1841
William Henry Harrison	Whig	1841
John Tyler	Whig	1841-1845
James K. Polk	Democratic	1845-1849
Zachary Taylor	Whig	1849-1850
Millard Fillmore	Whig	1850-1853
Franklin Pierce	Democratic	1853-1857
James Buchanan	Democratic	1857-1861
Abraham Lincoln	Republican	1861-1865
Andrew Johnson	Democratic	1865-1869
Ulysses S. Grant	Republican	1869-1877
Rutherford B. Hayes	Republican	1877-1881
James A. Garfield	Republican	1881
Chester A. Arthur	Republican	1881-1885
Grover Cleveland	Democratic	1885-1889
Benjamin Harrison	Republican	1889-1893
Grover Cleveland	Democratic	1893-1897
William McKinley	Republican	1897-1901
Theodore Roosevelt	Republican	1901-1909
William H. Taft	Republican	1909-1913
Woodrow Wilson	Democratic	1913-1921
Warren G. Harding	Republican	1921-1923
Calvin Coolidge	Republican	1923-1929
Herbert C. Hoover	Republican	1929-1933
Franklin D. Roosevelt	Democratic	1933-1945
Harry S. Truman	Democratic	1945-1953
Dwight D. Eisenhower	Republican	1953-1961
John F. Kennedy	Democratic	1961-1963
Lyndon B. Johnson	Democratic	1963-1969
Richard M. Nixon	Republican	1969-1974
Gerald R. Ford	Republican	1974-1977
James E. Carter	Democratic	1977-1981
Ronald W. Reagan	Republican	1981-1989
George H.W. Bush	Republican	1989-1993
William J. Clinton	Democratic	1993- 2001
George W Bush	Republican	2001-

CREDITS

This book was researched, developed and made possible by the wonderful access afforded to all via the World Wide Web. In the spirit of the Freedom of Information Act the majority of images represented here were downloaded from some of the various sites listed below. Basic content used to create our text is also from selected internet resources. The following is a partial list of the many sites we visited that inspired this book. Any potential copyright infringements herein are purely unintentional.

http://www.whitehouse.gov
http://www.ibiblio.org
http://www.politicalresource.net
http://lcweb2.loc.gov
http://pre1900prints.com
http://www.si.edu
http://lcweb2.loc.gov
http://www.usflag.org
http://www.americanpresidents.org
http://www.npg.si.edu
http://www.gliah.uh.edu
http://www.ipl.org
http://memory.loc.gov
http://educate.si.edu
http://www.presidentstrust.org
http://helios.insnet.com
http://www.mtco.com
http://www.historyplace.com
http://cybersleuth-kids.com
http://www2.lib.udel.edu
http://www.csuchico.edu
http://www.researchbuzz.com
http://www.11-sept.org
http://jccc.afis.osd.mil
http://www.jsc.nasa.gov
http://home.nycap.rr.com
http://www.law.ou.edu
http://www.nara.gov
http://grid.let.rug.nl
http://gi.grolier.com
http://creative.gettyimages.com
http://www.photolibrary.fema.gov
http://grin.hq.nasa.gov
http://www.infoplease.com

Addditional Credits
Richard Richter, consultant
J.D. Reichelderfer (www.hotadz.net), Design and Production